THE PUZZLE OF YOU

CONNECTING YOURSELF—A PIECE AT A TIME DURING THE TEEN YEARS

BY KASIA GUTIERREZ & CHRISTA PRUSS

The Puzzle of You; Connecting Yourself—A Piece at a Time
During the Teen Years

© 2021 Kasia Gutierrez and Christa Pruss

This book is available at special discounts when purchased in quantity for educational purposes or for use as premiums, promotions, or fundraisers. For inquiries and details, contact the publisher at confidencecoaches4kids@gmail.com.

ISBN: 978-0-578-99167-2

Cover and interior design by Liz Schreiter

We dedicate this work to our husbands, kids and students.

Jay and Nate: thank you for supporting our dreams and taking on all the responsibility of the family during our work seesions. Your dedication and selflessness will always be appreciated.

To Isabelle, Jackson, Katelyn, Carter and Jeffrey: you have inspired us to learn and do better in all areas. Parenting you has been, and will always be, our greatest privilege.

To our students: thank you for trusting us, and your willingness to be vulnerable enough to learn and grow. We love you all!

CONTENTS

WELCOME

You made it—welcome! We are thrilled you are here. In these pages, many of the struggles and challenges you will face as a teen and young adult are unpacked. You may have been given this book by a well-meaning, dorky adult in your life, and you may be wondering if this will be as lame as you expect it to be . . . no worries! This is not another textbook about the changes your body is going through. (Insert gag reflex here from one of our own teen daughters). Give us a chance. We are not your moms; instead, consider us your own personal coaches.

This is the book *we* needed when we were your age, something to help navigate the struggles of middle school, high school, and beyond. Through digging into and dispelling the lies we were told and have come to believe, we hope you will develop the confidence to walk through these years being 100% true to who you are. Come along with us as we discuss the importance of a positive mindset, healthy relationships, and the impact perseverance will have on your life. Find your favorite gel pen and comfy spot, and get ready to hear the truth about who you were made to be. It might be a bumpy ride. You may have to fight feelings of doubt and discomfort, but we are here with you, as you put together the pieces of *The Puzzle of You*.

You may notice, sometimes we refer to skills that may sound familiar. Terms like "self-awareness", "self-management," and "responsible decision making." Starting to feel like you're in a health class? Yes, we are educators, and we love all things called "Social and Emotional Learning." The thing is, this is an area that's not just a checkoff-box your teachers have to teach. This is the area of school and learning that we all desperately need to focus on, to be at our best. Researchers who've been focused on self-awareness for way longer than us have identified five key areas—we will uncover all five and link real life situations to them. Hang with us; it will be worth it.

In each section, there will be opportunities to journal and reflect on your experiences, feelings, and goals. Your inner voice is important, so take time to listen to your mind and heart as you respond to the prompts, thoughtfully and honestly. Thank you for being authentically who you were made to be. Let's get started.

SELF-AWARENESS

"KNOWING YOURSELF IS THE BEGINNING OF ALL WISDOM."

ARISTOTLE

"TO MASTER YOUR EMOTIONS

IS NOT TO SUPPRESS THEM.

IT IS TO PROCESS THEM WITH DILIGENCE

AND EXPRESS THEM WITH INTELLIGENCE."

KAM TAJ

BE AN EMOTIONAL DETECTIVE: KNOW YOUR FEELINGS

How well do you know your body? We know what you are thinking, "Please don't go there!"

> **Here is the deal:** your body helps you to understand what you are feeling and thinking.

We have to be aware of our emotions in order to know if we are in the right frame of mind to react to a situation. The physical responses you experience are tightly connected to your emotions. Body cues are the speed of your heart beat, the heat or chills you may feel, the heaviness in your heart, or the pit in your stomach. We've all had situations where we felt our body was reacting pretty strong to a situation. For Christa, she tends to get red and splotchy, while Kasia feels like her heart is going to beat out of her chest. Get to know yourself. It is important to listen to what your body is trying to tell you. What is your body feeling, and what is the reason behind the reaction?

Visualization is a strategy we *love* to engage in. We want you to think of a recent emotional experience. It could be a time you were happy; a time you were mad; or maybe even frustrated. How did your body feel? What was your body doing, to let you know you had strong feelings about the situation? Was your heart beating fast? Butterflies in your stomach? Was your face flushed red? It may seem cheesy, but it's important to listen, notice, and wonder about what your body is trying to tell you.

Here are some helpful tips for understanding and identifying your emotions:

TIPS FOR SUCCESS

1. ACKNOWLEDGE YOUR BODY CUES
2. BREATHE
3. NAME THE EMOTION YOU ARE FEELING
4. ATTEMPT TO UNDERSTAND THE WHY BEHIND THE EMOTION.
5. SET YOUR EMOTIONAL INTENTION: NAME AND VISUALIZE THE EMOTION YOU WANT TO FEEL

EMOTIONS AND MINDSET, FIXED VERSUS GROWTH

Have you ever had a time when you were faced with a new situation, and you told yourself, "No way! I am just not good at this" or maybe even, "I'll never be as good as . . ." Or maybe you head into a new experience full speed ahead, thinking, "I may not know how to do this yet, but I can't wait to try!"

Let's try to understand the truth about mindset and how to go from a fixed mindset to a growth mindset.

A mindset is a lot like a theory or belief you hold about yourself in relation to your intelligence or ability to learn new things. Usually, we either have a growth mindset or a fixed mindset. Growth mindset is the belief you have in your ability to learn and the ability to improve your intelligence through effort and perseverance. A fixed mindset is the belief that you are the way you are, either intelligent or not, and even when you work hard, it's unchanging.

There is power in believing you can become smarter through effort and time. When you truly believe deep down that you are capable, you are more willing to put in the hard work and the extra time. In turn, this results in growth, success, and confidence. For example, some people believe you're either a good writer born with a gift, or you're not. Those with a negative mindset, and who struggle with writing, believe they will never become a strong writer. They give up trying. But those with a growth mindset, who also struggle with writing, understand while some may be talented in that area, anyone can work hard and become a proficient writer. Maybe even a famous writer!

For people with a negative mindset, these beliefs can interfere with reaching your goals and feeling successful. But moving from a fixed to a growth mindset is easier said than done, especially when it comes to our tendency to compare.

We often struggle because we see our friends and classmates moving faster on assignments, raising their hands more, or making the team, which leads us to believe we are not smart enough or good enough for those same positive experiences. Research proves this type of thinking is unproductive and incorrect. In addition to comparison, the other problem with our mindset can occur from the environment we live in. Sometimes, well meaning teachers and parents tell you, at a young age, that you are smart. Sounds harmless right? While this is meant to be supportive, this can be a confusing message—the first time you make a mistake, or experience failure, your first thought may be, "I am a failure and I must not be smart."

Have you ever thought you are not good or smart enough? Maybe you think you will never be as good or smart as a friend? These can be dangerous and damaging thoughts because they cause stress, can lead to a lack of motivation, and, in extreme cases, lead you down a dark path toward depression.

Baseball star Derek Jeter once said, "There may be people that have more talent than you, but there is no excuse for anyone to work harder than you do." Thoughts like Derek's support a foundational positive mindset, allowing you to believe in yourself, achieve success and, in turn, become unstoppable.

It is natural to experience times of both positive and negative thoughts. It's important, however, to learn to become reflective of your thoughts and actions. Negative, or fixed mindset, thoughts allow feelings of guilt and sadness to hang around in your mind for too long.

The good news is your brain can easily be influenced and changed through your experiences. Not just emotionally, but it can actually change the physical makeup of your brain. When you have a growth mindset, you are willing to take on and learn from challenges, increasing your overall achievement. The coolest part is ANYONE can do this! With practice and intention you can rewire your brain to make connections between neurons and cells. Let's focus on practice. When you practice a skill over and over, whether it is academic, a sport, or a musical instrument, your brain is strengthening and connecting neurons, leading to growth and improvement.

Fair warning, though: with intentional growth mindset practice, you need to be willing to feel uncomfortable. Remember, you get to define yourself, not others. Strategies for this will come later on in the book. For now, we couldn't say it better than Stephanie Harvey: "Smart is something you become, not something you are."

CHRISTA'S STORY

I clearly remember as a second grader, my teacher asking me to leave the classroom when it was reading time. The other students would have the same book open to the same page, but all eyes were on me, as I walked across the room and out the door. It was clear that I was not smart enough to be a part of the class. I was mortified and embarrassed daily, which was the beginning of my fixed mindset, believing I was not smart enough for school.

I spent the next several years wanting to be invisible. Never wanting to be called on. Never earning grades that were good enough. I listened to teacher after teacher tell my parents at conferences that I needed to attend summer school or stay back a year. It was not until I met my 7th grade math teacher that I learned to believe that I had the ability to learn, and be just as smart as the next person. Ms. Tigh, with her coffee-cigarette breath, never gave up on me. She made me feel uncomfortable with her loud personality and strong belief in me. Daily, I was forced to step outside my comfort zone.

Little by little I saw my effort, time, and hard work pay off. I was learning and succeeding, and some of my success came from thinking positively about myself. It was this learning which created my desire to work harder and to spend more time working on my mathematical thinking.

SETTING THE INTENTION FOR SUCCESS

Today I will...

remind myself that emotions are not bad or good; they are human and necessary to learn and grow when processing experiences. I will separate my emotions from my character (who I am as a person). I will listen and pay attention to my body cues throughout the day, to understand how situations and experiences influence my feelings.

LEARNING IN ACTION

Take a moment to write or sketch your responses to the following prompts and questions.

Before you start, be aware you may need to ask someone you trust how *they* describe you; that can provide a jumping-off point, where you can agree or disagree with their characterization and use that to build your own list of personality traits and beliefs. It will take some major vulnerability to ask someone else's opinion, but it will pay off big time in your personal self-awareness.

Then, look at the prompts on the following page. Now that you are consciously thinking about who you are, how would you answer these questions?

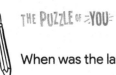

When was the last time I caught myself having a fixed mindset?

....

....

....

....

....

....

....

Do you feel you are born with a certain intelligence, or does it develop over time?

....

....

....

....

....

....

....

How are your emotions different when you are experiencing a fixed mindset versus a growth mindset?

....

....

....

....

....

....

"SELF—AWARENESS IS NOT SELF JUDGEMENT. IT IS LOOKING, AND SEEING, AND DISCOVERING WHO YOU REALLY ARE. SO, CHECK YOUR JUDGEMENT AT THE DOOR."

DR. CHRISTINA HIBBERT, AUTHOR AND SPEAKER

HOW WOULD YOU DESCRIBE
YOURSELF TO SOMEONE
WHO DOES NOT KNOW YOU?

ARE THE WORDS I TELL
MYSELF POSITIVE OR
NEGATIVE IN NATURE?

WHEN I LOOK IN
THE MIRROR: HOW
DO I FEEL ABOUT
WHAT I SEE?

THE IMPORTANCE OF KIND SELF-TALK

Self-talk matters. The way we talk to and about ourselves tends to become our reality. Negative self-talk impedes the super power of positive thinking. Let's face it, you are exposed to tons of negative thoughts from the media and it's tough not to absorb at least some of it. Then we have experiences listening to music, going to school, engaging in sports, and other social situations. You think you want to be just like everyone around you. You do not want to stick out; you want to just fit in. Before you know it, your thoughts have gone down a rabbit hole, and you are comparing yourself to your friends or people you admire. This is unproductive! When *we* start to feel ourselves falling into the comparison trap, we repeat the following quote by Theordore Roosevelt, "Comparison is the thief of joy."

All of us have different timelines. You learned to tie your shoes, be comfortable staying home alone, and, for some of you, learning to drive a car. You do this in your time, nobody else's. The truth is, negative self-talk and comparison lower your feelings of self-worth, interfere with friendships, and can create stress and anxiety.

Think back to having a growth mindset. Remember how we discussed intentional practice and focusing on trying to have a growth mindset instead of a fixed one? Your brain is an incredible muscle in your body that needs to be fueled by positive self-talk. What if . . . what if everyone believed in being true to themselves, thought kindly about themselves, and encouraged themselves during challenges and difficult times? You would feel safe and open minded about talking to yourself in a supportive way and taking on the world in front of you!

What if it seems like the only thoughts and self-talk you experience seem negative and unkind? Can you retrain your brain? Heck yeah you can! It's not just the physical change of neurons growing and connecting, there is also the change in your body that leads to the release of positive feel good chemicals, to help with your confidence. Remember the Disney movie "Inside Out?" Are you more "Joy" when it comes to your self-talk, or more "Sadness?" This begins with being reflective of your thoughts and memories that you focus on. Tune in to the voice in your head. Are you being too critical of yourself? How could you change your tune or rephrase your negative thoughts? As Karolina Kurkova said, "Talk to yourself like you would to someone you love." Let's take a look at how you can switch up your self-talk.

Instead of, "I'm not a math person, I've never been a math person," you can restate your thoughts and, instead, say, "I can learn math and ask questions." Or when you think, "I am not artistic or creative like my friend," you can rephrase it to, "I can spend more time watching YouTube lessons and practicing." Whether you are an athlete, a musician, or you just want to learn a new skill, focus on positive self-talk through encouraging words to yourself. You can do this. The time is worth it. Loving yourself allows you to love others and to be well loved.

"BE CAREFUL
HOW YOU ARE
TALKING TO YOURSELF
BECAUSE YOU ARE LISTENING."

LISA HAYES

KASIA'S STORY

Like many young girls, around the time I started high school, my body began to change. No longer was I the stick thin girl that could eat anything I wanted, and buy the size XS off the rack. Now, with the onset of puberty, my body had new curves, my skin looked like a pepperoni pizza, and I felt uncoordinated and frumpy. Top it off with huge braces and I looked nothing like any of the famous actresses of the time. I even had a senior boy say to me, "You know, you'd be really cute if you didn't have those braces." Ouch. I doubted the way I looked, dressed, and every single thing that came out of my mouth. Around that same time, I also began to doubt the one thing I loved doing and was sure I was good at: dance.

For as long as I could remember, I'd been dancing. It came somewhat easy to me, made me inexplicably happy, and I received positive praise and attention from it from my family and teachers. However, in this new body with curves and what felt like no equilibrium, I wondered if I was still a good candidate for the recent spot on my high school dance team. Who was I to wear those tight fitting outfits and get out there in front of over a thousand people at an assembly? Luckily, my mom had always been my number one fan. Her support of me as a dancer was strong and consistent. Any time I would start to doubt myself, she would say something about me being the best dancer she'd ever seen, or how my smile lit up a room, (even with my big braces). Although she has always been an exaggerator, and far from humble when it came to her children, I attempted with everything in me to believe her words. Her words formed the words I would tell myself: "I am a good dancer. I've been training for this my whole life. My body is fine the way it is. Go out there and show them what you've got."

Although it felt unnatural and fake at first, soon I was telling myself these things all the time. As an adult, I read a quote I remind myself of when I start to think negatively; "Change your thoughts and you change your world," by Norman Vincent Peale. I have to say, my positive self-talk about dance is a perfect example of this quote in action.

By focusing on positive self-talk, I was able to hit the dance floor and even made the All-City dance team as a freshman and, eventually, All-State as a senior. I don't mention these accomplishments to brag, but to bring up a point about how influential our thoughts are. Sometimes, I think about if I would have continued to believe the negative thoughts and self-talk instead of the positive? Would I have given up something I love? Could this have led to other decisions that reinforced the negative feelings I had about myself? I'm grateful for a mom blinded by love and admiration, who spoke positivity into me when I needed it most. Her words became the mantra in my head that helped me push through during this strange time and believe in myself again. The best part was, I actually had it in me the whole time! I just needed my mom to help bring it out.

LEARNING IN ACTION

Take a moment to write or sketch your responses to the following prompts and questions.

How do you handle thoughts that are not serving your mind or heart?

....

....

....

....

....

....

....

....

Think about how you would respond to a friend who described themselves in a negative way.

Would you tolerate it? How would you respond?

....

....

....

....

....

....

....

....

....

Consider why you are so quick to judge yourself harshly. Why do we do it to ourselves?

....

....

....

....

....

....

....

....

....

....

Talk to yourself like someone you love. List three positive qualities about yourself and place them on your mirror, your binder, or your locker, to read every time you need a positive reminder.

SETTING THE INTENTION FOR SUCCESS

Today I will....

pay attention to the reflective thoughts I have. When they are negative, I will restate my thoughts in a positive way. For example, instead of, "I am so stupid for failing this test," you could say, "I am so disappointed about this test. I don't like how this feels. Next time I will do more to prepare."

SELF-CONFIDENCE

"WHEN YOU HAVE CONFIDENCE, YOU CAN HAVE A LOT OF FUN. AND WHEN YOU HAVE FUN, YOU CAN DO AMAZING THINGS."

JOE NAMATH

SELF-CONFIDENCE: BELIEVING I CAN DO BIG THINGS!

The standard dictionary states that self-confidence is a feeling of trust in your abilities, qualities, and judgement. We'd like to add that when you have self-confidence you have positive thoughts about yourself *and* start to trust your abilities, which provides a feeling of a sense of control. It's important to know, our self-confidence can change depending on the environment or situation we find ourselves in. Part of self-confidence is understanding your strengths and weaknesses and trusting in your potential.

THE CONFIDENCE TO TAKE RISKS AND STEP OUT OF YOUR COMFORT ZONE.

This is one of our favorite topics! It's scary and intimidating, and yet so thrilling! Sometimes when things are exciting, but also scary, we tend to avoid them. We can't count the number of times we resisted stepping out, and, boy, do we regret it. It's hard to know at the moment, but positive risks are definitely worth it. There is a reason you have the desire to step out of our comfort zone. If you can feel it in your heart, then it's up to you to say yes, or no thank you.

Consider a goal, or something you've wanted to explore for a long time. Do you believe in what you want to do? When you believe in it, and it's a positive step, you should do it. "Wait!" we hear you saying. "Every time I feel this way, I should do it?" No. What you need to do is consider if the benefit of taking the risk will outweigh the scary feelings experienced before you take it. Our feeling is, if it's in your heart, you will probably be disappointed if you don't take the risk. You can't go back and rewind the story that has already happened. You can write the story from today on what you are hoping to achieve.

Think about this: risks are usually tied to big goals we have for ourselves, but they can be smaller, too. Some risks are connected to goals like making a team or taking a big test. It's scary at the moment, but the interesting thing is when you do it, the feeling of accomplishment afterward tends to outweigh the feeling of nerves in the beginning. Want to start stepping out of your comfort zone? Remember this: don't overthink it. If we know we want to do something, we need to go for it. Be like Nike. . . Just do it! Overthinking your every move is much like a hamster running in a wheel over and over, going nowhere. If you want to do big things and accomplish big dreams, you have to learn to be comfortable with being uncomfortable.

We are frequently uncomfortable trying to navigate social media and feeling uncertain. However, we feel strongly about helping you to understand yourself and be successful, so we are going for it and learning everyday. A little progress goes a long way toward feeling successful.

One thing to look out for, though: there can be a misconception sometimes. For instance, you might think if you're going for a big goal that you're not happy with your life in some way. That is not necessarily true! When you take a risk because of a goal, it doesn't mean that the status quo is not okay. It just means you see potential in something bigger. You may not make it the first time, but keep going and keep pushing. The more practice you have at taking a chance, the more comfortable you become with that uncomfortable feeling that comes with stepping out of your comfort zone.

  ## KASIA'S STORY

One of the big things many middle school students strive for is the comfort of being surrounded by friends at all times. Social connection is THE THING that means more than most anything else. Fear of missing out is a struggle in the middle school years! For instance, when I was offered the opportunity as an eighth grader to ride a bus to a high school across town to take dance classes, I was torn.

The school was a magnet high school for the performing arts. There were some of the best dance instructors available at the school. I actually was going to be able to take classes from an instructor from Oregon Ballet Theatre. However, the catch was I would miss out on lunches and afternoons with my friends at school. What would that mean for my friendships? Would I miss all the latest couple's news, or would my "relationship" with my middle school boyfriend be in jeopardy? There was a lot to consider, but my heart told me this was the right opportunity and risk for me to take.

It turns out, all is not lost when missing out on three hours of the school day in eighth grade. My friendships stayed intact, that boyfriend and I ended up staying together and dating for a couple years in high school, and I got to experience the most rigorous and challenging dance classes of my life. Taking ballet lessons from an OBT instructor, introduction to African Dancing, and a broadcast journalism class, gave me the confidence to head into my high school years ready for a challenge. I'm grateful my parents pushed me to take this risk, and I didn't overthink it and miss out.

SETTING THE INTENTION FOR SUCCESS

Today I will...

acknowledge the areas I excel in and look for
something I improved upon from the day before.

"OPTIMISM IS
THE FAITH

THAT LEADS
TO
ACHIEVEMENT.

NOTHING
CAN BE DONE

WITHOUT HOPE
AND CONFIDENCE."

HELEN KELLER

BEING OPTIMISTIC AND THE POWER OF POSITIVE THINKING

Where would we be without this magical super power?! We aren't kidding when we call it a super power, either. We are huge believers that having optimism and thinking positively is an intentional choice with the ability to dramatically change your life for the better.

If there is one thing that continues to propel us forward, it's our intentionality to choose positivity. What does that mean exactly? Does that mean I'm never allowed to feel sad or be in a bad mood? What about when my friend totally lets me down and all sorts of negative things come to mind? Absolutely you are allowed to be upset or sad and feeling our emotions is part of being human! The last thing you want to do is stuff down the hard emotions you are experiencing. You just don't want to stay there.

Choosing to focus on positive aspects of experiences helps us to learn lessons we can apply to future hard situations. It gives us hope, and helps us move forward. Not only that, but our positivity is a choice directly linked to our happiness. Yep. You read that right. Positivity is backed by science.

In a famous Harvard study on happiness, researchers found that "Forty percent of our happiness comes from the choices we make." When we intentionally make choices that lead to happiness, like positive thinking, it is life changing. There are other things we make choices about, such as health, relationships, and school, that can lead to happiness or even unhappiness. But as the famous Roman emperor and philosopher Marcus Aurelius said, "The happiness of your life depends on the quality of your thoughts."

For you, this could look like experiencing hard situations, and, when ready, focusing on what the hardship is teaching us. Processing the difficult experiences we go through, or, experiencing grief, while still choosing to find the positive lesson, helps us to experience trials that help us grow.

The reality is, positive thoughts and experiences don't just happen. We have to train ourselves to expect them. In our experiences, when we continually focus on positivity, we tend to attract positive situations to us. Interested in changing the course of your day? Try positive visualization. What is positive visualization, anyway? It sounds a bit strange. We understand, and if we hadn't experienced the positive benefits ourselves, we wouldn't bring it up.

Positive visualization is where you go into situations expecting positive outcomes, but it's not just hoping for the best. It's actually forming a mental picture of your experience. What are you wearing? Who is with you? What do you want to happen? This needs to be as clear as a movie in your head. When we've had a particularly difficult week, taking an extra ten minutes before jumping out of bed and engaging in a visualization is SO worth it. We use this time to thoughtfully visualize our day going smoothly, and honestly, it really makes a difference. It's amazing how when we expect positive outcomes, we tend to experience them. This is because we are ready for them, and more likely to recognize them. Try setting your thoughts for a positive day and see what happens.

Another way to experience positive outcomes is to influence others with your positivity. Positivity is contagious, and that's a contagion you want to spread. Don't let your environment or the tone of the environment influence you. Be an influencer and don't take on the negative vibes of others. You want to set the vibes in the room. Kobe Bryant said, "The most important thing is to inspire people so that they can be great in whatever they want to do." Inspiring them to be positive is a great start in the right direction toward greatness.

You may be thinking, "But I don't always feel positive" or "I barely can get through the morning, let alone infect others with my positive vibes." We have all been there, and, when you're as old as us, you tend to have plenty of reasons to lack positive thoughts. Here are some ways to flip the switch to positivity:

Find your person: The person you can talk to who listens, understands, and extends encouragement. (This is not someone who helps you throw a pity party). The biggest aspect of this person is they don't judge you, but they also call you out when you are being unnecessarily negative. They have high standards and expectations for you because they care about you.

Focus on gratitude: We could write a whole book on gratitude practices and the life changing outcomes for individuals who practice them. For now, start simple. Start with finding three things you're grateful for. Big or small things work. Good hair days, a rockin' dinner, or a special person or teacher in your life . . . all are a great start to getting out of a funk.

> "A PESSIMIST SEES THE DIFFICULTY IN EVERY OPPORTUNITY; AN OPTIMIST SEES THE OPPORTUNITY IN EVERY DIFFICULTY."
> WINSTON CHURCHILL

Focus on others: In a video we posted to our YouTube page *Confidence Coaches 4 Kids*, we discussed the need to use our special spy goggles to look out for others in need. It's almost impossible to remain down or negative when you're intentionally attempting to help others. Get the focus off you, and put it on someone who could use some kindness. Who looks like they're feeling down, or simply dropped their binder, or may need some extra encouragement? Reach out and change their day. Another way to focus on others? Connect with those you are grateful for and take the time to thank them. After all, "Feeling gratitude and not expressing it, is like wrapping a present and not giving it," according to William Arthur Ward.

Advocate for yourself: Talk to an adult you trust. Tell them you're feeling down, or could use encouragement. This means you will need to be prepared to answer the question, "What do you need?" As educators, we attempt to check in daily, but don't wait and tell that teacher how you're feeling. Need a hug? A little extra time or a walk to the restroom? Communicate! This helps the adult to check in, and also helps them to extend grace (or sometimes helps others like friends or other teachers extend grace, too).

Dance: This is our favorite strategy! We use this in our houses with our kids when they are grumpy. Works every time. Things to remember when you choose to dance: Music must be loud; sing along at the top of your lungs; and you need to dance like nobody's watching.

SETTING THE INTENTION FOR SUCCESS

Today I will...

expect good things to happen and be on the lookout for the positives, or find the lesson in each hardship.

SELF-AWARENESS: A CALL TO ACTION

So why do we need to be self-aware? Without truly knowing ourselves—our thoughts, our emotions, and our reactions—we tend to lack control in our response to situations. We just react without thinking, or get into situations repeatedly, which are difficult for us to process or handle. We have to know our triggers to effectively know ourselves.

Really, the only thing you can control is your effort, beliefs, and your attitude. If you aren't self-aware, how will you know where you stand, or where you want to go in life? The truth is, we have no control over anyone else but ourselves. When you take time to know and understand yourself, you are setting yourself up to be more proactive with managing your reactions in situations. This will lead to a feeling of self-control, and assists us with the development of positive self-management.

So what? Begin to consider your thoughts around the following questions:

- What do I think about gender?
- What do I think about politics?
- As I learn new things, am I willing to change my mind?
- Can I accept others who believe differently?
- Is there a lifestyle or belief system I can't accept? Why not?

The process of self awareness begins with knowing yourself and your beliefs. Understanding yourself is one piece of the puzzle, leading to a complete picture of who you are.

SELF-MANAGEMENT

"IT'S NOT WHAT HAPPENS TO YOU BUT HOW YOU REACT TO IT THAT MATTERS."

EPICTETUS

"LIFE IS TEN PERCENT

WHAT HAPPENS TO ME

AND NINETY PERCENT

OF HOW I REACT TO IT."

CHARLES SWINDOLL

REGULATING MY ACTIONS

Regulating your actions is what the grown ups in your life call "self-control." What is self-control? This is the skill of controlling your emotions, desires, and behaviors, especially in difficult situations. This does not mean stuffing down your feelings or ignoring them. To effectively regulate yourself, it's crucial to process these feelings, and move forward in a way that feels safe. This is easier said than done, and it will take practice.

Think back to the information regarding identifying body cues and naming our emotions from the previous section. When you're in a situation and you can quickly determine the emotions you are experiencing, the next step is to be intentional about your reaction. You can't take back your immediate reaction or outbursts during hard situations. Yes, we all lose it at times, but you can prepare for hard things and choose your reaction. It may be awkward, but sometimes you may need to completely walk away from the situation. Separating yourself for a time may be the only way to avoid a bigger mess than you want. What do you do in this situation? Here are some strategies:

- Acknowledge the clues your body provides you.
- Identify the emotion you are feeling.
- Consider possible reactions to the situation you are facing, including the way you typically react when deep in this emotion.
- Anticipate the consequences of the reactions to which you are prone. Will they help or be harmful to you?
- If needed, walk away and find a place to process the situation. This can be alone or with a supportive and trusted person.

LEARNING IN ACTION

Take a moment to write or sketch your responses to the following questions.

How do you typically react during hard situations? Describe a recent experience when you felt angry or left out. Be specific regarding your actions.

....

....

....

....

....

....

....

What words did you use?

....

....

....

....

Did you stay in the situation or leave?

....

....

....

....

....

How did your body react?

....

....

....

Would you respond the same way if this situation happened again?
Why or why not?

....

....

....

SETTING THE INTENTION FOR SUCCESS

Today I will...

remember I am responsible for my reactions and not
the situation. There will always be hard things, and the
only thing I can control is how I respond to them.

"LET US MAKE OUR FUTURE NOW, AND LET US MAKE OUR DREAMS TOMORROW'S REALITY."
MALALA YOUSAFZAI

{ AVOIDING THE ROADBLOCKS TO ATTAINING YOUR GOALS }

When you first learn about setting goals, it doesn't seem that complicated. We tend to think, "I'll just think about what I want, and then that's my goal." Well, that's a start, but it's not exactly all there is to it. In reality, there is much more to it. When we are excited and eager to accomplish a goal, it feels like we are unstoppable. That's why it might surprise us when there are roadblocks that we didn't see coming. Times when we are lacking motivation, struggling with perfectionism, or feeling defeated by failure can quickly make us feel unsuccessful at attaining our goals, and even steer us off course.

MOTIVATION MINUTE

Take a moment to write or sketch your responses to the following questions.

Do you have a strategy to move from unmotivated to motivated in order to get things done?

....

....

....

....

Do you remain motivated and dedicated when "it" gets hard?

....

....

....

....

Do you have a goal? Big or small that you are working toward?

. . . .

. . . .

. . . .

. . . .

How do you support your future self?

. . . .

. . . .

. . . .

MOTIVATION TO ACCOMPLISH YOUR GOALS

When you love your hobby or sport, you are willing to work hard, sweat, fail, and try again. This is the activity you feel you were born to do. You are ready to spend every waking hour focusing on this area of your life. But how do you show up in other areas of life that are not as enjoyable at the moment?

At this point in life, you may not be aware of the impact your work ethic has on your future. To be fair, it's hard to envision yourself as an adult. You may be an eternal optimist and just expect things to work out when it comes to your goals. Optimism is great, but so is the reality of planning and working hard.

We understand some areas will get more effort than others, especially during certain times in your life. However, we've found that when you focus your efforts in one area, typically this focus spreads to other areas of your life. When you are motivated to improve your free throws or beat the next level of your video game, you become disciplined to continually play, practice, and improve. Without realizing it, you have become disciplined through this practice and have unlocked your potential in a way you didn't anticipate. The best part is, this discipline and momentum can spread to other areas of your life if you are intentional.

How do you get there? What if it's something you don't want to do. What can you do to help yourself put in the work that is needed? It starts with reflection. When you get in a situation that you do not want to be in, like a writing assignment, you intrinsically know when you have given it your all, and when you haven't. So, if after engaging in a task or situation, you aren't feeling proud of your effort, this is an indication you probably need to step it up the next time. At some point, you have to dig deep and look inside. Intrinsic motivation is your part. Extrinsic motivation comes from the people in your life that care about you and are cheering you on.

Mariia, age thirteen, shares her feelings on trying to stay motivated:

"I will be honest here. Sometimes, it's hard to stay motivated. Sometimes, you just don't feel like you will finish what you started. In my experience, the greatest reason is laziness. I decide that I can do it later, it doesn't matter anymore, or some other thing to avoid doing it. And to be honest, I sometimes give up, which isn't a really good thing. But something that I sometimes think of is a simple question: "Why did I even start this?" It makes me think about why I even set that goal, started a project, or did something that requires dedication. Another thing that requires motivation is something that you know you have to do but don't want to. For example, my 2020 seventh grade year has started off with online school instead of in-person school. This did not make me happy and I needed to stay motivated every day. Something I think might help to think about is: "How can I make the most of something I don't enjoy?" There's always something you can enjoy, even when it's hard. And you don't have to like it, just know that it will be worth it at the end."

THREE STEPS TO MAKING MOTIVATION A HABIT

 Motivation is supported by routine. Remember in school when you learned about the five W's? Who, What, When, Where, and Why. Think through this when building a ritual for whatever the activity is. Who is supporting your routine? When is this routine happening? WHY are you building this routine? You get the idea. Here are some specifics:

- Sitting in a specific place to do your homework
- Wearing a certain t-shirt to practice shooting hoops
- Eating a consistent food before you leave for school

You may not feel motivated for the activity or event, but, if you have created a specific ritual, then you are preparing your mindset to get started.

 Your routine should be something that helps you to move toward your goal. If you are feeling sluggish or bored, notice what you are doing . . . probably laying on the couch or slouched over your desk. The opposite is true when you are feeling motivated. You are moving your body or doing something that is helping you to make progress toward your goal. So, create a routine that is simple enough to get you moving and to program your mindset into being ready. It could be as simple as holding/carrying your basketball around the house for five minutes before heading out to practice shooting free throws.

 Follow the same pattern or routine each time. Your routine becomes a habit that is connected to that activity. It signals your brain naturally to be ready because it is thinking, "This is what I do before I start _____."

"MOTIVATION IS WHAT GETS YOU STARTED AND HABIT IS WHAT KEEPS YOU GOING."
BRENDON BURCHARD

LEARNING IN ACTION

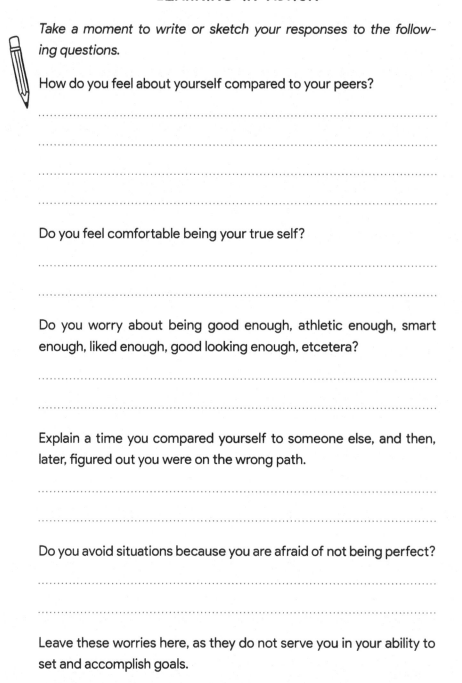

Take a moment to write or sketch your responses to the following questions.

How do you feel about yourself compared to your peers?

....

....

....

....

Do you feel comfortable being your true self?

....

....

Do you worry about being good enough, athletic enough, smart enough, liked enough, good looking enough, etcetera?

....

....

Explain a time you compared yourself to someone else, and then, later, figured out you were on the wrong path.

....

....

Do you avoid situations because you are afraid of not being perfect?

....

....

Leave these worries here, as they do not serve you in your ability to set and accomplish goals.

WHAT IS PERFECTIONISM?

Believe it or not, the path you travel before you get to perfectionism can have many pros and cons. When high standards are used as motivation to push yourself, they can be an important part of reaching your goals. It's when your standards shift over to the realm of perfection at all costs, that we have a problem. It is common for many of us to struggle with perfectionism in a particular area.

Perfectionism can cause stress and anxiety. Often, you have a vision of how you should look, or how you expect your schoolwork to turn out, and the final product does not match with the picture you created in your mind. This struggle often leads to negative thoughts, and the feeling of failure or unworthiness. Why? Why do you do that to yourself? Perfectionism interferes with confidence and impacts your learning and performance.

We are very familiar with the struggle of striving for perfection while competing against friends. What's tricky is that we don't always do this knowingly. Friends are often drawn together by similar interests and work habits. Sometimes, this can lend itself to a hidden competition, which leads to doubting ourselves or feeling resentful toward others. Think about swinging on a swing set . . . push and pull, push and pull, as you pump your legs to go higher and higher. We find ourselves pushing to get ahead or being pulled back by others who are interfering with our picture-perfect outcome.

What does perfectionism look like? Do you feel like the only acceptable grade to earn is an A? Are you crushed if you don't make every team you try out for? Do you insist on being the best at everything you attempt? Well, that is what perfectionism looks like. In addition, more often than not, students struggling with perfectionism are wound up (worried or stressed out about failure or time); critical of themselves (using negative self-talk); and not having fun. Sometimes, we are so deep in our perfectionism that things like schoolwork don't get completed, due to the fear it won't match our perfect vision. What are the perfectionism messages you are listening to?

Feeling the need to be perfect can weigh on our hearts and minds. When our brain feels overloaded or even empty, our heart feels heavy and we often freeze because we do not know how to proceed without being guaranteed perfection.

  ## CHRISTA'S STORY

I shared earlier that I struggled to read. I had a teacher who felt it was acceptable to ask me to leave in front of all of the other students as they got their reading books out because I needed extra reading support. I struggled to read for a long time because I could not read perfectly. I tried to hide in my seat and pray that my teachers would not call on me because I could not perform like my classmates. This second grade experience impacted me all the way through high school. I always enjoyed sports and being active, but I NEVER played a sport in middle school or high school for fear of not being perfect or good enough.

If I could not do anything as well as the people around me, I wouldn't do it. I feel so much regret today. I watch my students and my own children push themselves at tryouts even when they are nervous, continue to play in the game even when they make a mistake, and while I feel proud, I am always overcome with a sting of sadness for myself. I hear and see their teammates and friends encouraging them, their coaches mentoring and supporting them, and I always think about how I missed opportunities because I suffered from perfectionism. On the flip side, I am the obnoxious mom and teacher in the stands encouraging and focusing on the positive learning opportunity when something doesn't go well. Why? Because you all are out there DOING IT! To be perfect is to be unrealistic. If everything is perfect, there are no learning opportunities for growth or to achieve full potential. Be you, make mistakes, and work to be better than you were yesterday.

What are some ways you can celebrate the positive steps you are making toward your goals, while focusing on progress and not perfection? Is there someone in your life you notice doing this, too? What have you seen them do?

THE "F" WORD: FAILURE IS A GREAT THING

In a recent conference we attended, Brandon Fleming (speaker and author) said, "Failure is not your destination, it is only your process. Failure is the one thing most people do not do well and it can have the potential to paralyze you or move you forward."

It's important not to believe the stories our failures tell us, and, instead, to focus on the learning opportunities they provide. We put pressure on ourselves wanting to achieve our goals and tend to feel defeated, discouraged, and beat ourselves up with negative talk when our plan doesn't go as planned. Oftentimes, we ask ourselves, "Why me? Why didn't I make the team? Why does it always happen to me?"

What would you say if someone told you they hoped you failed? Just consider your reaction if a trusted friend, mentor, or parent said this to you. It feels unexpected and even a bit insulting, but the truth is, we must fail in order to grow in most situations. We learn from our experiences, as they provide us with wisdom to share and inspire others.

We find our students struggle with this concept when we share this piece of advice with them. Even crazier is when we celebrate their failures. As teenagers, why do you dislike these "talks?" What are you afraid of when you hear talks on failure and perseverance and learning opportunities? What is the turn off? Why does it feel so frustrating?

Failure feels scary and never feels good with the moment. For some, when you think about failure, it may bring up feelings of rejection and possibly shame. We understand the feeling of worrying about what other people think about us when we fail, too. We aren't going to lie; in those moments, it feels big and painful. We want you to know that these horrifying failures will evolve in your mind with time. You won't always feel like your world is over or wake up feeling disappointment when you think of your failures.

In time, you will be able to identify the lesson learned or you will know how to better handle the situation differently next time. In fact, over time, you may even be able to connect with some of the cool things about failure.

BENEFITS OF FAILURE

- Builds character
- Creates opportunity . . . a different outcome or opportunity may present itself instead of your original plan
- Provides great teachable moments . . . learn from those moments
- Teaches perseverance
- Instills courage
- Requires motivation . . . if you don't like the outcome, then change it. Use your failure to motivate you to try better or do differently next time

The greatest impact is in how you recover from failure; this is the most valuable part! Acknowledge the discomfort and physical feeling of having a pit in your stomach. Now what?

GETTING THROUGH FAILURE

You have to put the failure and disappointment into perspective. If you're worried about what others are thinking, remember, usually people are not talking about you. They are worried about themselves.

Choose your mindset . . . is this experience a problem to be solved or a life sentence?

Continue to practice—don't give up! You may be one step closer to achieving your goals.

Use your sense of humor. It's important to avoid taking ourselves too seriously. It's truly healing to laugh at yourself.

Google famous people who experienced failure and went on to be huge successes.

Above all, remember, get back up and try again. We were made to do difficult things in life, and you are stronger than you think you are.

"THERE WOULD BE NO INNOVATION OR CREATIVITY WITHOUT FAILURE, BUT IT IS HARD TO FAIL BECAUSE WE FEEL SO VULNERABLE."

BRENÉ BROWN

SETTING THE INTENTION FOR SUCCESS

Today I will...

focus on the goals I have set for myself. I will find motivation when it's lacking. I will not be derailed by perfectionism, distracted by comparison, or afraid of failure.

"IT IS HARD TO FAIL,

BUT IT IS WORSE

NEVER TO HAVE TRIED

TO SUCCEED."

THEODORE ROOSEVELT

FLEXIBILITY AND RESILIENCE

Being flexible is not an easy task. We get so caught up in how we think our lives should go that we just can't shake our expectations. The truth is, life is not always what we expect or think it should be. How can we pivot when things don't go as planned? Even harder, how do we pick ourselves back up and create a Plan B when we've been knocked down? This is hard! When you've had a sleepless night, walking yourself through every detail of the way you think things should go, it can be very disheartening to have things change. You will need to show resilience and adaptability more than ever. We give power to what others say. We start to believe it . . . However, things can change.

WHEN HAVE I
EXPERIENCED
A SITUATION
THAT WENT
COMPLETELY
DIFFERENT THAN
WHAT I EXPECTED?

DO I SHOW
RESILIENCE, WHEN
THINGS GET HARD?

HOW DO I REACT
WHEN THINGS
DON'T GO AS
PLANNED?

RESILIENCE: WHAT IS IT?

Since we've discussed the "F Word," naturally we need to discuss resilience next. What is it? Seems like a buzz word educators use, right? Resilience is when you fight against the urge to let the difficulties and challenges in your life take over and bring you down. Instead of giving up, you find it in yourself to continue on. Resilience is not some magic quality some of us are born with. It takes work, and, honestly, most of it is mental work. It's an intentional reframing of your thoughts and natural tendencies to give up, and instead rise up and try again. If we were to narrow down the main factors that play into resilience, they are acknowledging the pain and discomfort of hard situations, attempting to control your emotions, and reframing negative thoughts into productive ones.

How do we build resilience when we have failed, or feel the difficulty in moving on? When you're in the situation, or what we lovingly refer to as "the pit," you will need some specific ideas for how to move forward. It won't be easy, but to start, look for the good in your circumstances rather than feeding your disappointment. It's important to understand that building resilience isn't easy. It's really like a muscle you have to build up. It takes time and repetition and a commitment to get stronger.

Here are some ways you can build resilience:

- Ask yourself, what is this experience teaching me?
- Make a plan of action to try again.
- Chat with a friend or family member to brainstorm.
- Write in a journal if you're feeling the pain from losing someone special.
- List reasons why you are good enough just the way you are.

CC4K'S STORY

To be completely honest, we wish we had more experiences in which we showed resilience as teens. Unfortunately, we were the types of adolescents that tended to avoid hard things, or resisted our dreams to move forward. We were okay with sitting in our comfort zones, not taking risks. However comfortable we were, we weren't totally satisfied. This is probably one of the reasons we are so passionate about supporting young people today. We don't want to let fear of failure lead *you* to future regret. As we've embarked on this journey as speakers and authors, there have been some hard things. It's always hard when you see others succeeding in the areas you are striving for, and you don't understand why you aren't in the same position. We've applied for opportunities we were sure we were perfect for, only to get the short, two-sentence rejection email. We've made awesome plans to support athletes at the University of Oregon, started work on our presentation, only to be postponed and then eventually cancelled all together. It stinks. Every. Single. Time. But, we believe in what we do. We continue to dream big and work hard, because our dream is too good to give up on. Friends, we encourage you to also dream big, fail, and get back up and try again. Your dream is attainable if you stick with it.

LEARNING IN ACTION

Take a moment to write or sketch your responses to the following questions.

Think back on a time you failed in the recent past.

....

....

....

....

What did you learn from that failure?

....

....

....

....

Write a note to your past self prior to that time.

....

....

....

....

What advice would you give yourself now that you have moved past the disappointment?

....

....

....

....

SETTING THE INTENTION FOR SUCCESS

Today I will...

remember to be flexible when things don't go as planned. There is always a Plan B I can come up with. My goals can still be achieved through my resilience and commitment.

ORGANIZATION IS KEY TO GOAL ACCOMPLISHMENT

Yep—what the grown ups in your life have told you is true. Organization is an essential skill for success. In particular, organizational skills will keep you on track to make sure you are making progress toward your goals. In fact, when you think of self-management as a whole, organizational skills like planning, time management, prioritization, and follow through help you create systems to attain your goals. We can already hear you: "But I'm just not good at organization. I was born without that skill." We get it! I (Kasia) am not organized by nature. However, over the years, I've developed some skills that have ensured I actually keep my job, and happen to keep my little humans alive, if just barely.

You may have heard the saying, "Failure to plan is planning to fail." In this section, we want to provide some tips and tricks to help you in your journey to become more organized.

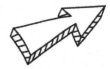

"WITH ORGANIZATION COMES EMPOWERMENT."
LYNDA PETERSON

ORGANIZATIONAL TIPS AND TRICKS

List making: Where would either of us be without this skill? There is something so satisfying about crossing a finished task off a list. Turns out, your brain actually releases the feel good chemical dopamine when you scratch something off your list. We love science!

Visual planners/calendars: Over the years, we've tried many different planners and organizational tools. Until recently, we didn't realize these tools had to be in our line of vision! The saying is "out of sight is out of mind" for a reason. Keep your calendar in a frequently visited area where you're sure to see it daily. We go crazy over color coding and using pretty pens and fonts, but, at the very least, you have to remember it to use it.

Whiteboards: This is connected to the list-making tip above. If you are prone to losing your lists (Kasia), you'll love using a big whiteboard. Use it to track your to do lists, chore charts, and your homework assignments (with due dates, please), all in one VISIBLE place.

Have a designated place for everything: Now we really sound like your grown ups! When you've planned ahead and have a place for your frequently used items like backpacks, laptops, or school work, you will save so much time looking for them. So, put your belongings right away, where they will be when you need them. Seriously, try it for a couple weeks. You're welcome in advance.

Backward planning and using sticky notes: This is specific to school work. Frustrated or overwhelmed with big projects with multiple parts? We like to start at the final product, work back, piece-by-piece. Start with the due date and work backward, assigning tasks to each week or day, ensuring enough time to complete a project

Timers: We live in a world *full* of helpful technology. We love us some timers. When we're feeling unmotivated to get started, we often will set a specific time for us to commit to working and set a timer. Use Alexa, your watch, or even your phone timer and commit to a short work session. Most times, we find when the timer goes off, we've hit a groove, and we aren't ready to stop working.

SETTING THE INTENTION FOR SUCCESS

Today I will...

choose two of these tips to attempt over
the next three weeks in order to increase the
self-management skill of organization.

SELF-MANAGEMENT CALL TO ACTION

Are you starting to get the gist of why self-management is so important in life? Honestly, we can't think of another area that supports success in so many areas of our human experience. When you manage your emotions and reactions, you keep your relationships intact. Your commitment to resilience in the face of failure leads to the accomplishment of your goals. Your ability to organize your life leads to way less stress, positive relationship support (just ask our husbands), and ability to get things done to attain your goals and dreams.

If you need to, reread this section. Identify the areas of self-management you struggle with, and those that are strengths. Commit to improvement in the areas you need it and continued excellence in the areas you are strong in. Understanding yourself enough through self-awareness and practicing strong self-management will lead you toward a deep understanding of others, as well.

SOCIAL AWARENESS

"TO EFFECTIVELY COMMUNICATE WE MUST REALIZE THAT WE ARE ALL DIFFERENT IN THE WAY WE PERCEIVE THE WORLD AND USE THIS UNDERSTANDING AS A GUIDE TO OUR COMMUNICATION WITH OTHERS."

ANTHONY ROBBINS

HOW DOES MY
ENVIRONMENT AFFECT
MY COMMUNICATION?

HOW CAN I
TELL HOW
OTHERS ARE
FEELING?

ARE MY REACTIONS
TO THINGS
DIFFERENT FROM
PEOPLE FROM
OTHER CULTURES?

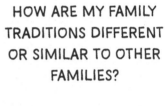

HOW ARE MY FAMILY
TRADITIONS DIFFERENT
OR SIMILAR TO OTHER
FAMILIES?

63

"LEARNING TO STAND

IN SOMEBODY ELSE'S SHOES,

TO SEE THROUGH THEIR EYES,

THATS HOW PEACE BEGINS."

BARACK OBAMA

EMPATHY AND SOCIAL AWARENESS

How do you feel when someone judges your actions or words in an unfair way? Wouldn't it be nice to have someone listen to you and attempt to understand your experiences? You don't need to completely understand someone else to show empathy. You just need to let them know you are there and listen without judgement. Some of the hardest situations in life would be less scary if you knew someone was there to support you. You may not understand someone else's reaction or feelings, but you can always support them and attempt to show respect for their point of view and reactions.

Empathy is the skill of attempting to understand others feelings, thoughts, and actions. To develop this skill, you may need to try to see them through a new lens, or imagine yourself walking in their shoes. Attempt to wonder how someone might feel in a situation or why they feel the way they do. How might their experiences have impacted them to feel or act as they are? True empathy happens when you engage in curiosity, just like you would with a good book or Netflix series. Seek to understand others and expose yourself to different world views to encourage your empathy muscle.

EMPATHY IN ACTION

Showing empathy to others can take many forms. As sixth grade teachers, we've seen some amazing demonstrations of empathy by our kids. Whoever said middle school kids are all about themselves clearly doesn't know there is more than meets the eye when it comes to you all. Empathy can look like a "cool" kid playing a game with "that kid" who has a difficult time making friends. Or, it could be seeing someone eating alone and choosing to invite them to sit at your table. Maybe it's noticing a kid who doesn't get any Valentine's grams and rushing to make sure they get one delivered the next day.

You know when you're listening to a speech and you can feel the stress and anxiety rolling off of the speaker? It's the intentional decision to encourage them throughout the speech with your head nods and smiles. Empathy might look like not sharing a picture or video on Instagram or Tik Tok, because you wouldn't want that to happen to you. The point is, you are taking the time to consider how someone else is feeling and do something to help them. This isn't just a random act of kindness or feeling sorry for someone. This is understanding situations where others are uncomfortable and stepping in to help, because you know you wouldn't want to be in the same spot.

LEARNING IN ACTION

Choose a picture above. Write about what you think the person is feeling or experiencing. How do you know, or what made you think about them in this way?

....

....

....

....

··

··

··

··

··

··

··

··

··

··

··

··

··

··

··

··

··

··

SETTING THE INTENTION FOR SUCCESS

Today I will...

be curious and ask questions and seek to understand
rather than make assumptions from my own experiences.

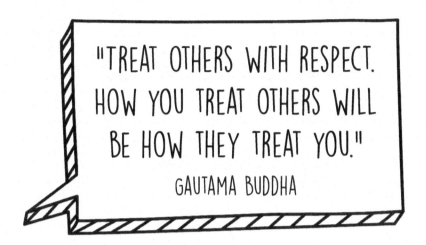

"TREAT OTHERS WITH RESPECT. HOW YOU TREAT OTHERS WILL BE HOW THEY TREAT YOU."
GAUTAMA BUDDHA

RADICAL RESPECT

Remember kindergarten, when you discussed the "Golden Rule?" The Golden rule states, "Treat others the way you want to be treated." Although it's not all encompassing in terms of respect, it's a start, and it feels like every school rule is based on this idea. When our interaction with others is rooted in respect, strong relationships are formed. We aren't referring to a feeling of intimidation or being afraid of someone. You can actually disagree with someone and still be respectful. True respect is when you have a high regard for someone. Maybe you respect their ideas about the world, or the work they have done to improve it. Sometimes respect looks like admiration, or looking up to someone. Sometimes respect is having enough self-management skills in your toolbelt that you can control your reactions to others.

How can we show our respect for others? It starts with positive interaction. In most cases, it's being aware enough to fight against harshness toward others, or aware of a lack of human engagement. To start, focus on listening and being present in the moment with others. People know when you are distracted or not listening. Just think of the times you're attempting to talk to your parents or a friend while they are looking down at thier phone. Do you get the vibe they are listening to you? Probably not. The thing is, being known, listened to, and understood is at the heart of our desires as humans. We want to be seen, but also really see others. We have a desire to be heard, and we grow from listening to others. Through being present to listen, and trying to understand others' perspectives, we can make decisions that benefit both others, and ourselves, while being thoughtful of their feelings.

LEARNING IN ACTION

Take a moment to write or sketch your responses to the following questions.

Consider a time when you have felt disrespected.

What did it feel like?

....

....

....

....

....

How did you react?

....

....

....

....

....

Did this person or group of people have power over you?

....
....
....
....
....

How do you think this impacted your response?

....
....
....
....
....

Can you identify a time when you failed to show respect to another person?

....
....
....
....
....

What would you do differently now?

....
....
....
....

SETTING THE INTENTION FOR SUCCESS

Today I will...

think about how my words or actions might impact
others. I will attempt to show others respect,
even when I feel differently or disagree.

APPRECIATION OF DIVERSITY

As we've grown, we have developed a deep appreciation of diversity and differences. For many of you, especially if you are white, you've had the privilege to grow up in an environment surrounded by people who look or think like you. Although this can be comforting at the time, you are missing out on the essential experience of being different from those around you. You see, we grow as people, when we are exposed to thoughts and experiences, different from our own. How can you develop critical thinking skills and truly understand what you believe to be true in this world, if you are only exposed to one world view or way of life?

You need to listen to others and learn from their experiences, with eyes and hearts open. As you walk the halls at school, or interact with kids in classes, look for and celebrate the differences you see. You will find many things, like family norms, are different all over. We encourage you to remember that just because something is different doesn't mean it's wrong. When faced with a person or idea different from your own, do you automatically feel defensive, or do you lean into curiosity and willingness to learn?

The most powerful thing you can do is stand up for a group of which you are not a part. In adolescence, with your desire to fit in, differences can become a source of conflict, and even lead to bullying. We believe if you witness bullying or hear a racial slur, you have a moral obligation to stand up for others (which can include telling a trusted adult). Remember when we said respect doesn't mean you never disagree? In this case, it means you may disagree but continue to treat others like the valued humans they are. This standing up to others will take on different forms. It doesn't matter HOW you do it; it just matters that you DO it. Don't buy into focusing on differences as a negative. Focus on how you would want to be treated. Wouldn't you rather grow and connect with others, rather than continue to support a divide?

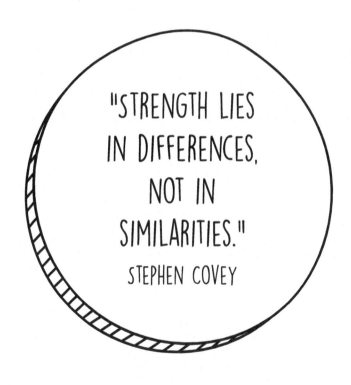

"STRENGTH LIES IN DIFFERENCES, NOT IN SIMILARITIES."
STEPHEN COVEY

LEARNING IN ACTION

Take a moment to write or sketch your responses to the following questions.

Have you ever caught yourself staring at someone who is different from you? Maybe you're intrigued, feeling discomfort, or just caught off guard by a new person. Maybe you're unconsciously telling yourself a story about who they are or what they are like.

Take a minute to ask yourself, "What made me feel this way?"

....

....

....

....

What was intriguing or made you feel discomfort?

....

....

....

....

....

Do the thoughts or ideas you have help build relationships or an understanding of others?

....

....

....

....

....

SETTING THE INTENTION FOR SUCCESS

Today I will...

be aware of my possible bias I have toward others. I will
identify it, and I will consider where it comes from.

UNDERSTANDING GROUP DYNAMICS

Group norms and dynamics can be hard to figure out, especially
when you are new to a group. The ability to read other's emotions
and relationships in a group is not an easy skill. However, over time,
this will help you to not only understand a group, but also its individual members. This does NOT mean you are required to change to fit
in, it just means you will understand reactions and communication
from others in a clearer way. For many of us, we are only familiar with
the norms of our own family or our close friend group. So, how do
you understand group norms and interactions, especially when you
are new?

When you go into new contexts or environments, attempt to anticipate how the social norms for communication and interaction may
be different than yours. Look for cues (body language, facial expressions, tone of voice) in others to identify emotions and respond
appropriately. Who is an influencer in the group? This won't always
be the most vocal person in the room. Some of the best influencers
are listeners first. You will spot them by how others will defer to them
and eventually ask their input. Look for how group members interact
with each other.

"WHEN PEOPLE TALK, LISTEN COMPLETELY. MOST PEOPLE NEVER LISTEN."

ERNEST HEMINGWAY

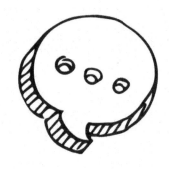

LEARNING IN ACTION

Take a moment to write or sketch your responses to the following questions.

Think of a group you belong to. Maybe this is a class you are in, a sports team, or your family.

Consider the relationships between the people involved. Below, sketch how members are connected. What do they have in common?

Who is more connected to each other?

....

....

Is there friction between any members?

....

....

How does this information help you as you navigate this group you belong to?

....

....

....

....

How is this group related to your authentic self? (The person you truly are).

....

....

....

....

SETTING THE INTENTION FOR SUCCESS

Today I will...

look and listen for cues in others in order to
attempt to understand the relationships and
expectations of groups I am involved with.

SOCIAL AWARENESS CALL TO ACTION

Social connection is essential to us as human beings. We are, for the most part, made to interact with others. When we feel connected, we feel understood. In addition to the feel good aspects of connection, when we are socially aware, we are more able to understand others. In particular, we can better understand perspectives different from our own.

So why is this helpful? It's a fact of life that you won't stick with one social group forever. When we are little, we start out connected to the people who raise us. As we age, we begin to connect with others outside our circle, like when we go to school, participate in an outside activity, or just venturing out into the public. As we increase our ability to understand others, and understand norms in different situations, we can be successful in a variety of environments.

Think of a time you were in a situation where you observed someone who seemed to lack understanding of the unspoken rules of behavior of a certain place. Maybe you were in a movie theater and a person in attendance was talking loudly over the movie. Annoying, right? Well, did you see a sign that said, "No talking during the movie?" Probably not. You just happen to be aware enough of the expectations of the environment. Take comfort, we don't always automatically understand the social rules of different places or groups. Social awareness is a skill we develop over time, and through experience with people different from ourselves. So, take a risk; step out of your comfort zone and strive to understand others and the world around you.

RELATIONSHIP SKILLS

"FRIENDSHIP IS THE ONLY CEMENT THAT WILL EVER HOLD THE WORLD TOGETHER."

WOODROW WILSON

"GOOD COMMUNICATION

IS THE BRIDGE

BETWEEN CONFUSION

AND CLARITY."

NAT TURNER

COMMUNICATION CREATES CONNECTION

From our experience as teachers, we know the kids we work with LOVE to talk. We can't remember a day we haven't had to wait for our sixth graders to finish up their conversations with a friend, as we are trying to start a lesson. Although talking with a friend comes pretty naturally, talking is just one area of communication.

Communication is a key ingredient in the ability to form and keep healthy relationships. Success in the workplace and at school, becoming a leader, and achieving long term happiness is determined by your positive relationships. What can sometimes happen, though, is communication can break down when we are feeling peer pressure or struggling with our self-management. Although you won't always be the best communicator in your circle of friends, it helps to "find your people." When we feel connected, we are not only invested in developing great communication skills, we also are comfortable to mess up and improve.

LEARNING IN ACTION

Take a moment to write or sketch your responses to the following questions.

You may love to talk with friends, or you may be more reserved. You may have a relative you can spill everything to, and one you clam up around. Think of a time when communication has broken down in one of your relationships. Maybe it's a time when you or a friend said the exact *wrong* thing to another person. You meant one thing, but something else came out instead.

Describe the situation and the reaction of the people involved.

What would you do differently the next time?

....

....

....

....

....

....

....

....

....

....

....

....

....

POWER OF CONNECTION

Oh, how we wish we would have known the value of finding your true people earlier in life. It would've helped us avoid a lot of fake friendships along the way. We heard somewhere that, "Your vibe is your tribe." This refers to the people who you can be yourself with. Who is your person or people that you can count on?

As a teen, you tend to think the more friends you have, the better you are. Being "popular" and well liked is like the gold star you wanted to earn when you were in elementary school. Really though, a million friends is not necessary. Now, instead of a quantity of friends, we think you should focus on quality.

Great friendships require time and effort, and too many friends is too much work. Find people who love and respect you for who you are. Even when your friends have a strange love for Harry Potter (Kasia). Or, for some reason, they may love all things camo (Christa). So, how do you know who your people—your tribe—are? They will not only accept you, but they will encourage you to be yourself. When you are yourself, and your friends or people around you say that you're too much, it's clear they are not your people.

Do the friends in your life encourage you, or do they cut you down whenever they can? You want to be around people that want to help you grow, and you should want to help them grow. Friends that are better than you in other areas should motivate you to be the best version of yourself, and not make you feel insecure. Friendships are reciprocal and mutually beneficial, like a two way street. You become more like the people you hang around, so choose wisely. Like Oprah says, "Surround yourself with only people who are going to lift you higher." We would add that you need to lift those around you higher, as well. Choose the friends that you are motivated to encourage, and, if they are really your people, they will do the same for you.

 KASIA'S STORY

Growing up, it seemed like I had a lot of friends. I was able to hang with a lot of different people from different social groups, and, for the most part, I was liked. In high school, I was in a group of friends that when all of us got together, there were around twenty of us. That made for some fun weekends! From the outside looking in, it would have seemed like I had a *ton* of friends. However, in that group, there were a only few who really knew me, and knew the real me.

These friends were the ones I could be vulnerable with about my home life. When I made a bad decision, they were the ones to call me out and remind me I was better than I was acting. When things were great or horrible, they were the ones I called or paged. . . Yes, back in the late nineties, I had a pager. The color was "cranberry" and it was awesome. We all had one and our own special codes, and we thought we were the coolest!! (You are probably so confused right now. It's okay. Ask one of the grownups in your life. They will know what I'm talking about.)

Thankfully, I'm still friends with this small, core group today. We've experienced over thirty years of friendship together, and we still get each other. I love how I can meet them for breakfast after being apart for months and months, and we can pick up like it was just yesterday.

These are the types of people you want in your life. If you don't have them yet, don't worry. Sometimes, the most amazing friends show up, when you're not even looking for them. After the core group from my school years, I was so surprised when I had another shot at an amazing friendship as an adult. Christa Pruss is my person now. The one who gets me, pushes me to be better in all areas of life, and who I can be completely vulnerable with. One of the best aspects of our friendship is we can own our nerdiness around each other. There is no story or experience embarrassing enough to result in one of us not accepting each other or laughing like crazy, together. We are there to pick each other up when one of us is down, and help each other see the possible lesson that could be learned. I'm grateful everyday for our friendship and this amazing adventure we are on together.

LEARNING IN ACTION

Take a moment to write or sketch your responses to the following questions.

What qualities do you appreciate in your friends?

....

....

....

....

What is something a trusting adult does that helps you to feel safe and connected?

....

....

....

Who is somebody that has positively impacted your life and helped you to be who you are today?

....

....

....

Write a letter letting those people know how much you value and appreciate your relationship.

Perhaps you can't think of anyone . . . This DOES NOT mean you are un-loveable or un-deserving of a close friendship. Prepare yourself for the kind of friendship you want. Dream a little, and then be ready when this friendship presents itself. Write a letter to your future best friend, the one you can be yourself with.

SETTING THE INTENTION FOR SUCCESS

Today I will...

be intentional regarding which characteristics are important to me in relationships. I will be sure to reciprocate those same characteristics to the people I value.

BUILDING TRUE RELATIONSHIPS

Fitting in versus belonging is a fascinating conversation to have with others. One of our favorite authors, Brené Brown, discusses this topic quite a bit. It got us thinking about how we have an innate desire to be with others and to not feel alone. We felt this way as kids and we still feel this way.

Especially in the middle school years, we tend to feel a need to never feel alone; always surrounded by others; even at the expense of our happiness. We have had many conversations with middle school students who have many friends but feel like they have no REAL friends at all. When we share this with our book groups, the kids shake their heads knowingly. Why? Because we all experience this same feeling. It may not always look or feel like it, but we do.

We go through stages in our lives where we work extra hard to not feel lonely or isolated. We will settle on friendships to avoid standing out. We want to blend in and not be noticed. Fitting in is not being your true self. Fitting in is molding your ideas, music and fashion choices, sports interests, and decision making, to be part of a group. Fitting in can also be giving in and accepting the identity your parents are trying to assign you. We want to please the trusted adults in our life, not disappoint them, and sometimes this can happen at the expense of our happiness and comfort.

We want to feel loved and valued in our families, so we will give into others' desires or dreams for us. For example, you may be "forced" to play the piano even though you have no interest and it never feels fun. We believe it is important to always try new things and give them a fair chance, especially when your parents believe it is important. However, after putting in the time and effort to try it out, we would encourage thoughtful conversations with the adults in your life about these activities. You should not have to be a musician to fit into your family; just like you should not have to dress a certain way to fit into your friend group.

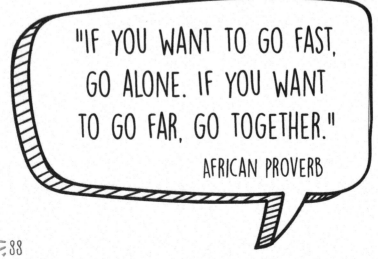

"IF YOU WANT TO GO FAST, GO ALONE. IF YOU WANT TO GO FAR, GO TOGETHER."

AFRICAN PROVERB

Belonging is different. It's the ability to be who you want to be, and also loved and accepted for who you are. We are all unique and different, even if we have many commonalities with our family and friends. Belonging is to be loved, appreciated, and valued for you. Thinking back to our middle school years, knowing what we know now, we encourage you to make being yourself a *norm* in the schools and communities you belong to. Instead of feeling like we need to fit in, let's focus on feeling like we belong. This is so much easier said than done. How do we break down the walls and barriers in our schools so the culture is built on acceptance and kindness? Even the "popular" kids feel worried about fitting in. It doesn't appear that way as an outsider looking in, but it takes a lot of sacrifice to keep yourself at the top. Working to stay popular can be exhausting and crush you on the inside. It is *never* worth it to be popular at the expense of others.

So, let's do it! Let's create change in our school cultures! Let's create change in our social media cultures! Let's embrace the uniqueness of others even when their interests do not match ours. Let's compliment each other, smile at each other, and be brave enough to be vulnerable with each other.

CHRISTA'S STORY

My middle school experience was at a junior high; seventh through ninth grade. I had moved to Colorado from California in the middle of my sixth grade year. I struggled with confidence and was extremely introverted. I had a hard time making friends. I remember being followed home by kids singing "Old McDonald Had a Farm" while calling me a snob. They interpreted my shyness for confidence. I was mortified, so when it came time for junior high, I was a mess. I wanted to fit it in. I didn't want to be alone. I was worried about eating by myself in the cafeteria. I met another girl named Brandy in one of my classes. I was grateful when she willingly started a conversation. We soon became friends, but my gut knew she should only be a school friend. I'm not sure how to explain it. I do not remember Brandy saying anything specific that put up a red flag in my mind, I just had a feeling. I wanted friends and needed friends, so I worked hard to ignore that feeling.

I remember her asking me to go to the mall. My mom dropped us off one afternoon, and we walked and talked and enjoyed our new independence as seventh graders. We had several items of clothes we took to the dressing room to try on for fun because neither one of us had enough money to buy anything. While in the dressing room, Brandy started putting clothes in her backpack. I was so freaked out! I couldn't believe it. Was this a joke? Was she really going to steal? I panicked. What was I going to do? I quickly came up with the idea that I needed to use the bathroom. I told her I would be right back. I hurried out of the dressing room.

My mom was there. I hadn't realized, but my mom had pretended to drop us off and then secretly followed us around the mall. When she saw my worried expression as I emerged from the dressing room, she knew something was wrong. I told her what was happening and that I had no idea what to do. She quickly helped me devise a plan. I hurried back into the dressing room to let Brandy know that my mom had come early because she needed a few things and I happened to run into her on my way to the restroom. I told her she better not risk stealing anything because my mom was there and would kill me if she knew what we were doing.

Most reliable comment ever! Always blame your parents when you need to get out of an uncomfortable situation. We have all been in trouble and we all can relate to being busted by our parents and avoiding lost privileges and consequences, so use the excuse whenever needed. You will be surprised what it can get you out of.

Also, the stress and worry this situation caused me was not worth it. I know that now as an adult, but as a kid, not so much. We are wired to connect with others and we will make sacrifices to connect. Any relationship that causes you to detour from your comfort level is not worth it. You will belong! You do belong! You will find your people, you will feel loved, you will feel happiness and you will feel safe…remember this when you are stuck fitting in rather than belonging. Belonging is coming!

LEARNING IN ACTION

Take a moment to write or sketch your responses to the following questions.

How do you know you truly belong to a group?

....

....

....

Identify a group you feel most comfortable with.

....

....

....

Why do you consider yourself a true member?

....

....

....

....

SETTING THE INTENTION FOR SUCCESS

Today I will...

work to create change in my school culture and
social media feed, by embracing the uniqueness
of others, and working to be brave enough to be
vulnerable with my own feelings and thoughts.

> # "PEACE IS NOT THE ABSENCE OF CONFLICT. IT IS THE ABILITY TO HANDLE CONFLICT BY PEACEFUL MEANS."
> ## RONALD REAGAN

SEASONS OF FRIENDSHIP

We are created as social beings who crave connection with others. Some of our most meaningful connections can be in the form of friendships. Friendships are important but sometimes we feel insecure in them. There are times when we feel we are only liked and accepted because of a perceived value we bring to a friendship. Sometimes we worry that friends might find us annoying or they enjoy their other friends more. We have people we are tight with and we fear we may lose them. Normally, this feeling comes from insecurity. What happens when you feel that you are the only one giving in a friendship and not receiving anything in return? How would you know how to recognize it?

Are you feeling like you are walking on eggshells around a friend and trying extremely hard to be who you think they want you to be? If you are feeling unsure or possibly judged about who you are, and wondering if you won't be liked due to something you wear or enjoy, this is a one-sided friendship. The truth is, however, this is normal.

Interpersonal dynamics vary from relationship to relationship. Honestly, you probably can't avoid this, but you do want to be aware of it. We encourage you to reflect on who you are, and, when you feel ready, to be yourself! Sometimes we are in these relationships because we are trying to survive a new experience like middle or high school, or different social situations. Eventually, though, you will have the courage to step away from these relationships and be who you were meant to be. In our experience, these types of friendships will end. Initially, it will feel uncomfortable and even lonely, but you will have grown from this experience, and, in your gut, you will know it's the right choice.

The thing is, many friendships have seasons, and different seasons of life result in us being closer to certain friends. Friendships grow and change over time, and you may even find yourself needing space from each other. In our experience, when there is space between you and your friends, sometimes you will find your way back to each other in a different season. It's perfectly normal to worry about friends making stronger connections with other friends than you, but there's not much you can do about it. Separations of friendships happen organically as you change and grow over time. Luckily, this usually happens slowly and helps us get used to the distance. Typically, it's not usually a big blow out fight. If it feels uncomfortable, reach out to an adult, a parent, or a teacher to work through your feelings and process. Love yourself and value yourself. Don't forget that there is something special in you that attracts others and don't forget we don't always give ourselves enough credit. Enjoy and take care of your friendships; value them and also understand they will change.

LEARNING IN ACTION

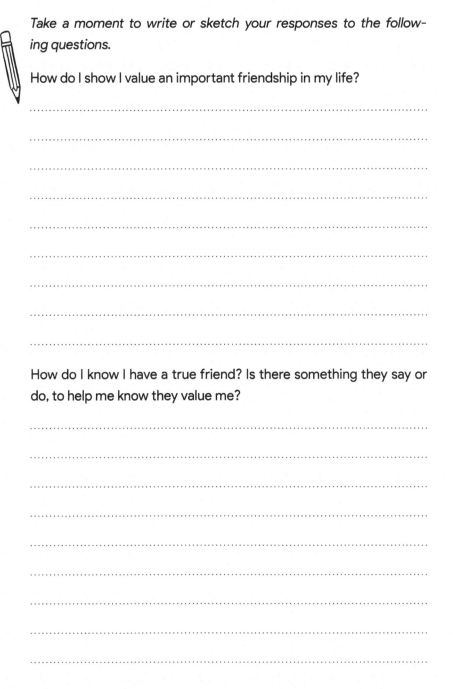

Take a moment to write or sketch your responses to the following questions.

How do I show I value an important friendship in my life?

....

....

....

....

....

....

....

....

....

How do I know I have a true friend? Is there something they say or do, to help me know they value me?

....

....

....

....

....

....

....

....

....

CONFLICT

Having hard conversations, especially with friends, is extremely difficult. Have you ever felt like someone is mistreating you, attacking you, or targeting you? Are your friends talking about you in a hurtful way, and maybe you worry about their feelings, even though your feelings are also being hurt? Or you may be experiencing one of the worst situations: others are saying things about you that are not true.

It's important for you to know that you need to take a moment to reflect, and not react, when you're in these situations. Actually doing this in the moment is hard; it doesn't feel logical or even doable because we feel emotional when in these situations. If you want to resolve conflict positively, and have a chance at retaining the relationship, you have to intentionally choose to do this. The first step is to just stop. Refrain from talking. You don't need to respond right away. There is no shame in waiting to respond so you are not responding in anger. This is your opportunity to think, "What is the best way to respond"?

Next, as Stephen Covey says, "Seek to understand the other person before being understood."

You may be thinking, "Huh? Why would I want to understand them? They are hurting me and in the wrong . . . Man, this is so tough." However, the truth is, you need to pause and try to understand what they're trying to communicate before worrying about what *you* want to communicate. Maybe this is not even about you. What is the person thinking or feeling? You remember your mom's advice about trying to put yourself in their shoes? It's actually a wise move. Think about the reason your friend might be speaking this way. Honestly, If they are just trying to be mean, then they are not your friend.

Or, could it be that there's something else going on? Now it's time to reflect on your own actions. Yes, that's right, you may have something to do with this conflict. Don't deny it; own it. We all make mistakes, and It doesn't make you weak to admit it. After you've had a chance to consider your part, then it is time to respond. When you do, remember, no one is perfect. Always respond from a place of love and grace.

Everyone wants forgiveness. Focus on your facial expressions. Are you glaring at them while you talk? Attempt to "fix your face," and it will help bring down the wall between you, and soften your friend. Respond out of love, even when you're not currently feeling it. This takes practice and often is easier said than done. When we've experienced this with friends, it helps to think about how you would want to be responded to if you messed up. But also, if this is not working, and it's a repeated thing, then take time to re-evaluate the friendship. There are some relationships that just aren't worth keeping. Most of the time, love and compassion will lead you to a place of resolution, especially as you are figuring out where you fit in.

  ## KASIA'S STORY

It's true that no matter how close you are with someone, conflict is bound to happen. We are all different, from different backgrounds, and we have different triggers and emotions around certain situations. In college, I met some of my best friends. It's funny how sometimes you just feel like certain people get you, right from the beginning. One of these friends of mine is Shelby. In college, we always had a blast together, county line danced with the best of 'em, and many nights ended with our stomachs hurting from laughing so hard. So, after a particularly hard season in my early twenties, I found myself in need of a roommate, and Shelby was first on my list. We moved in together the first year we had teaching jobs and things were great. We grocery shopped together, spent Sundays grading, and always had time to watch movies together in the evenings. However, eventually, the dynamics in our relationship changed a bit. I began dating someone, and I started to hang with him more and more. I ended up being away from our apartment a lot, and our movie watching and hanging time dramatically decreased. I knew she wasn't thrilled about it, but instead of talking with her, I avoided the conversation. This led to distance between us, and eventually we parted ways. The bummer was, it was awkward and tense between us for a long time. It wasn't until we talked about it much later, that we were able to process the pain and disappointment we both felt. I had the opportunity to apologize and let her know how much she meant to me. How much time did we waste not talking about the problem? Thankfully, we are still friends, but that was a hard season to get through.

My advice would be to just talk it out right away. Stay calm, attempt to listen to the other person's perspective, and prioritize the friendship. You'll be much better off if you do. And that guy I was so focused on hanging out with? He was history within a few months. Positive friendships always take priority over loser boyfriends or girlfriends. Lesson learned.

LEARNING IN ACTION

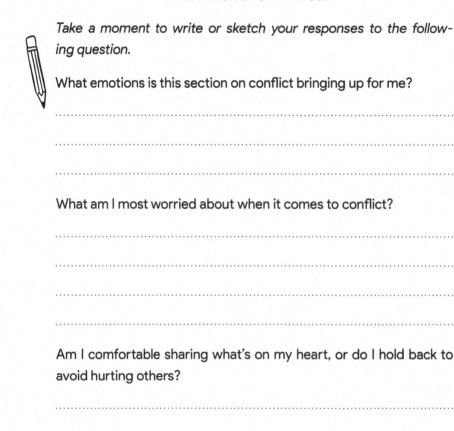

Take a moment to write or sketch your responses to the following question.

What emotions is this section on conflict bringing up for me?

....

....

....

What am I most worried about when it comes to conflict?

....

....

....

....

Am I comfortable sharing what's on my heart, or do I hold back to avoid hurting others?

....

....

....

....

Is there a way to prepare for hard conversations that has helped me?

....

....

....

....

....

SETTING THE INTENTION FOR SUCCESS

Today I will...

remember to refrain from responding quickly if faced with conflict. I will pause and listen to my mind and heart before I address the issue.

TEAMWORK MAKES THE DREAM WORK

"BETTER TOGETHER!"

"TWO HEADS ARE GREATER THAN ONE!"

"TOGETHER EVERYONE ACHIEVES MORE!"

We've all heard these sayings at one time or another. Sometimes we feel the power of collaboration energize our thoughts and feelings, and other times we feel stuck when working with others. Relationships help us grow, and growth is crucial to our success. Knowing our people and building strong relationships helps us to feel safe and willing to take risks as well as persevere. On the other hand, there are times when working with a group can feel painful, but these are moments to lean into and embrace. Why? Because learning to engage with others that frustrate you or causes struggle helps you become stronger in the long run. Help your future self by listening, watching, and being open to different perspectives. We are made to do hard things and this includes relationships. All relationships take work. Relationships can rock, while also being rocky. There are ups and downs in friendships.

REMEMBER THESE TIPS:

* COMMUNICATE YOUR FEELINGS.

* LISTEN!

* REFLECT ON THE IMPORTANCE OF THE FRIENDSHIP.

Communicate your feelings. Listen. Reflect on the importance of friendship. Find an adult you can trust and process your thoughts and feelings in order to mentor you during a tough time.

It's important for us to have a team atmosphere in friendships and relationships. We need this in our classrooms too. We are better when we are together, pushing each other's thinking, while picking each other up. We understand it's not easy to work with everyone, and there is no doubt people will get under your skin at times. Sports teams have to figure this out and so do we. Be intentional to look for others' strengths and understand your strengths and weaknesses. We grow more when we are exposed to new or different thoughts— you don't always want to be with like minded people. Groups made up of different people with different thoughts help us grow! After all, how will our ideas, considerations, and challenges be expanded if we only associate ourselves with people just like us?

"THE STRENGTH OF THE TEAM IS EACH INDIVIDUAL MEMBER. THE STRENGTH OF EACH MEMBER IS THE TEAM."
PHIL JACKSON

RELATIONSHIP SKILLS: CALL TO ACTION

As humans, we crave connection and belonging. At the core of this need, is our ability to establish and maintain healthy and fulfilling relationships. While we talk about "finding your people," healthy relationships aren't always with people who look like you, believe your beliefs, or have a similar background. Successful relationships require the necessary skills to connect with people different from ourselves. This is possible, and doesn't require you to conform to others' expectations or peer pressure.

One way to develop strong relationship skills is to intentionally seek to understand individuals different from yourself. This will not happen if you only surround yourself with people exactly like you. Scary right? What if someone disagrees with you? Even worse; what if they disagree with you in front of others and you feel called out? To be honest, this is hard for adults too. There is no way to improve at this type of interaction, than to expect it to happen, and respond from a place of empathy.

Consider the world today, and the events of the last few years. Many people feel more divided from others than ever before. It used to seem as though cooperative discussions and coming to a mutually beneficial decision was the main goal. Now, whether scrolling on social media or watching the news, when others feel differently about an issue, or don't agree with our plans 100%, we assume that they are wrong. We challenge you to attempt to listen and understand others' perspectives, in an effort to create connection and healthy relationships. Fair warning; this is harder than it sounds. Many adults (including us) struggle with this concept. However, we wouldn't ask you to do anything we knew you weren't capable of. We encourage you to lead the change we need, and focus on relationship building, instead of "winning" an argument. It will be difficult, but most things worth doing usually are.

RESPONSIBLE DECISIONS

WHY DID I DO WHAT I DID?

WOULD I MAKE THE SAME DECISIONS AGAIN?

WHAT ARE THE CONSEQUENCES OF MY DECISIONS? BOTH POSITIVE AND NEGATIVE?

WHAT DO I DO NOW?

HOW DO MY DECISIONS IMPACT OTHERS?

"IDENTIFY YOUR PROBLEMS

BUT GIVE YOUR

POWER AND ENERGY

TO SOLUTIONS."

TONY ROBBINS

PROBLEMS AND SOLUTIONS

Identify a problem in your life you feel responsible for. The one that leaves you feeling sick to your stomach, and you can't stop thinking about it. Maybe you embellished as you were gossiping with a friend, leading to hurt feelings or a conflict with another friend. Your gut will tell you you've messed up. Before you move on, though, please remember, who you are isn't solely defined by your actions. You are human and you *will* make mistakes . . . Now carry on.

The best thing you can do, is to own up to your part in this situation. Don't attempt to backpedal or talk about all the reasons you are validated for reacting the way you did. Always tell the truth and admit to the ways you dropped the ball. This truly leads to resolution, while lying typically leads to a bigger problem. Think about the possible solutions that could either help or hinder your attempts to solve the situation. Ask yourself, "What do I do now?"

Once you have identified your part, begin to think about all aspects of the problem. Why is this situation a problem? What are the consequences? Who else is affected? As I move forward with a decision, whose voice isn't represented? This will help you to think deeper, and you will use your social awareness and relationship skills to identify a solution to help all parties. While your problem isn't solved yet, focusing on possible solutions and their consequences will help you decide on the best course of action. You will feel proud of your ability to independently make decisions that offer the best options for all people involved. This is how you strengthen relationships with those around you, as you develop confidence in yourself.

```
SETTING THE INTENTION FOR SUCCESS

                    Today I will...

        acknowledge my problem and choose a way to
         process it, as I begin to consider solutions.
```

PROBLEM SOLVING:
TAKING RISKS EVEN WHEN UNCOMFORTABLE

This is one of our favorite, yet scary, topics. Sometimes when things are scary, we tend to avoid them. It's hard to know at the moment, but these risks are definitely worth it. There is a reason you have a desire to step out of our comfort zone. Do you believe in what you want to do? When you believe in it, and it's a positive step, you should do it. You need to ask yourself if the benefit of taking the risk will outweigh the scary feelings before you take it. Our feeling is, If it's in your heart, you will probably be disappointed if you don't take the risk. You can't go back and rewind the story that has already happened. You can write the story from today on, focused on what you are hoping to achieve.

Risks are usually tied to big goals we should have for ourselves, but they can be smaller, too. Some connect to goals like making a team or taking a big test. It's scary in the moment, but the interesting thing is when you do it, the feeling of accomplishment afterward always outweighs the feeling of nerves in the beginning. Want to start stepping out of your comfort zone? Remember this: don't overthink it. If we know we want to do something, we need to just do it.

Overthinking your every move is much like a hamster running in a wheel over and over, going nowhere. If you want to do big things and accomplish big dreams, you have to learn to be comfortable with being uncomfortable. As mentioned previously, we are uncomfortable everyday trying to navigate social media and feeling uncertain, but we are going for it and learning everyday. There can be a misconception sometimes, that if you're going for a big goal, then you're not happy with your life in some way. Not true! When you take a risk because of a goal, it doesn't mean that the status quo is not okay. It just means you see potential in something bigger.

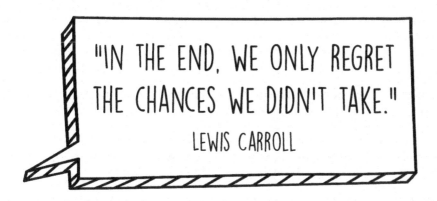

"IN THE END, WE ONLY REGRET THE CHANCES WE DIDN'T TAKE."
LEWIS CARROLL

 KASIA'S STORY

I will say, taking risks as a kid wasn't something I tended to go for. I didn't work crazy hard to have the perfect double turn for the dance team, or study like crazy for the perfect grades. I wouldn't lose it emotionally if everything wasn't just how I'd planned it. I typically did just enough to get by. Now, as an adult, I recognize my lack of risk taking was directly linked to my perfectionism. I simply wouldn't let myself take chances to do things when I knew I might fail. I wasn't pushed to do things out of my comfort zone by my family, so I kept to activities and classes I knew I could be successful in. Honors English was a no brainer, so I enrolled. Upper level math was a definite no.

My local state college was easy to get into, so yep, that sounds good. The college out of state? There's a story there.

I grew up dancing, and I felt confident as a kid, so I would take calculated risks in this area. However, there was one area in which I lacked confidence in; my technical dance skills. So, when on a college visit trip to Boise State University, I knew immediately that I would not take the risk of trying out. Even after the awards and accolades I'd received growing up, I knew I couldn't hang in that environment. Why, you ask? Those dancers had some of the best technical skills I had ever seen. These girls were busting out triple turns and switch leaps during warm ups.

I immediately felt like an imposter. Who was I on this trip out of state, thinking I could dance in college? That's for people who grew up in studios competing since the age of five. We could only afford studio classes for a handful of years before I left. I wish I had a different end to the story, but it turns out I just didn't go for it. I stayed in my hometown, lived at home, and remained firmly in my comfort zone. My college experience was still enjoyable, I cheered at my local university, and I got the degree I studied for. Of course, those choices got me to where I am today, and I'm grateful. However, how many times do we let our fears get in the way of taking risks to accomplish our goals? Who knows, I may have missed out on an amazing adventure of growth in Idaho.

LEARNING IN ACTION

Take a moment to write or sketch your responses to the following questions.

Refer to the problem you identified in the previous section. Make a t-chart identifying three solutions on one side and three possible outcomes on the other side.

Which solution would best fit this problem?

....

....

....

....

What are you nervous about?

....

....

....

....

....

What are possible consequences when working through the problem?

....

....

....

....

Now, implement the solution.

SETTING THE INTENTION FOR SUCCESS

Today I will...

avoid responding to problems like I am a
victim. Instead, I will acknowledge my part as I
implement a solution to move forward.

EVALUATION AND REFLECTION

The opportunity to stop and reflect is one you don't want to miss.
You've made the t-charts about a problem and a solution. You've
even gone forward and implemented the solution. What now? You
must take the time to evaluate how it went, and think about people
who were affected by the situation. This is crucial, as it helps you
make responsible decisions in the future. Many times, we have made
a decision and simply moved on, happy to have any conflict or stress
behind us. This is normal! However, sometimes our decisions will
lead us to experience even more discomfort or stress. What do you
do when this happens? Below are a few actions that are helpful.

"DIFFICULTY CREATES
THE OPPORTUNITY FOR
SELF—REFLECTION AND COMPASSION."
SUZAN—LORI PARKS

STRATEGIES TO ENCOURAGE REFLECTION ON DECISIONS

Commit to regular journaling- If you don't already have a journal for your personal thoughts, ask a grownup in your life to immediately take you to the store to buy one, or order one online. We mean it! Do it now. Journaling is an excellent way to get your thoughts out in a safe and productive way. Read through your writing regularly as you assess the impact of your decisions.

Bullet journal- This is a specific type of journal that allows you to draw, write, and track your goals and feelings regarding everyday situations. There are so many varieties on Amazon. Check it out if you want an artistic way to express your thoughts.

Talk it out with your person- It is imperative to have someone you can talk to about your decisions. When we talk aloud as we reflect, we understand ourselves in a different way. Also, having a trusted person giving you honest feedback will assist you as you engage in honest self reflection, in order to make future decisions.

Get physically active—There is something so powerful about clearing your mind as you move your body. Endorphins are released through exercise, and your stress starts to melt away. Freedom from this stress on your body encourages thinking *and* reflection (even when you don't feel like it).

LEARNING IN ACTION:

Take a moment to write or sketch your responses to the following questions.

Consider the decision you identified in the previous section.

What are the positive or negative consequences of my decision? How did it impact others?

....
....
....
....
....
....
....
....
....

Why did I do what I did?

....
....
....
....
....
....
....
....
....

How did it make others feel?

....

....

....

....

....

....

....

....

If I were to experience a problem like this again, what would I do differently?

....

....

....

....

....

....

....

SETTING THE INTENTION FOR SUCCESS

Today I will...

have an open heart and mind about monitoring the impact my decisions and actions have had on others.

"THE TIME IS ALWAYS RIGHT TO DO THE RIGHT THING."
—MARTIN LUTHER KING JR.

PERSONAL, MORAL, & ETHICAL RESPONSIBILITY

First identify what the concepts of personal, moral, and ethical responsibility mean to you.

Think about the MLK quote; not everyone agreed with his stance on individual responsibility and change. How do you feel when other people have different ideas about what is right or wrong?

We would argue that we move towards a more balanced, harmonious community, when we have varying thoughts and perspectives. What do you do if your perspective is different from others? Do you pause and listen, or do you "defend" yourself? Has this caused you conflict? After listening to others, have you avoided stating your own beliefs? Has this caused you conflict?

The Golden Rule Connection: it is important to communicate your truth, but equally as important to not feel the need to persuade or change others and their truth. You have to be okay with your own definition of morality and right versus wrong, and know others may not agree with you. That is okay. Be true to your beliefs while attempting to see other's perspectives. Does this mean you need to convince others to agree with you? No way! It's not your job to change their minds.

Another important thing, is to always stand up for others when you see injustice. Maybe this is a bullying situation. Someone might be gossiping in your presence. You will know when it's wrong, because you will feel it in your gut. You know what we mean. Feelings like butterflies in your stomach, getting sweaty, or just an overall feeling of being uncomfortable are big clues. (Remember the section on body cues? Here it is again.) When in doubt, trust the signals and signs your body is giving you to act.

You may be thinking to yourself, "Well, that's easy for you to say. You've already found your people and you're confident in speaking your truth. I will never have friends again if I disagree with my friends or stick up for someone weird." The truth is, it's never easy. Even as an adult, we can hesitate. Here's what we know for sure: when you don't stand up for others, and let the moment pass by, you will regret it later. Doing the right thing is usually not easy, but it's always worth it.

LEARNING IN ACTION

Take a moment to write or sketch your responses to the following questions.

What is your definition of right and wrong when it comes to decision making?

....

....

....

....

....

....

How did you form this opinion?

....

....

....

....

....

....

Did it come from your parents or upbringing?

....

....

....

....

....

How do you know if your decisions are right or wrong?

....

....

....

....

....

....

What do you do when confronted with different beliefs than your own?

....

....

....

....

....

....

SETTING THE INTENTION FOR SUCCESS

Today I will...

seek to understand others' perspectives, while
staying true to my beliefs, when my thoughts
about right or wrong differ from theirs.

THE LAST PIECE OF THE PUZZLE

Are you ready to be a person of action? Someone who understands how the pieces of The Puzzle of You come together?

There will always be challenges to overcome. Some will be small and others will feel overwhelming and maybe even unmanageable. What can you control? Will you be ready to make decisions to help you advance toward your goals and dreams? Will you be ready to accept a challenge and to grow stronger? Will you always feel positive? To be human is to feel struggle, and have moments of negativity and defeat. Acknowledge those moments, embrace those moments, reflect, take time to think, breathe, talk, dance, write, or do whatever helps you to release negative energy. And then, take a step forward. Reach into what you know and learn from those moments.

  ## CHRISTA'S STORY

Middle school and high school were hard. As I mentioned in previous stories, I didn't feel like I belonged and I felt too far behind to even try to fit in because friendship groups seemed so tight already. When the time came to apply for college, I remember feeling like this was my chance. My chance to be me. Wherever I went, no one would know me. No one would know I was so painfully shy and insecure. I could walk onto a campus and be the Christa I was meant to be. I felt like I had nothing to lose because everything and everyone was new. So, I did it. I applied to a small college in another state because it was a fresh start. I was tired of feeling like I was not good enough or worried about what others thought. My stomach was constantly full of butterflies and I typically had the awkward presence of red creeping up my neck and cheeks from feeling discomfort inside, but I introduced myself to new faces and was intentional about becoming outgoing. The best part, most everyone else felt just as nervous. Maybe not for the same reasons, but we were all new and trying to figure ourselves out. I am grateful I took that risk and I am grateful that I chose to be intentional. I had moments of discomfort at first, but, over time, I could breathe easier and had new friends by my side. Icing on top of the cake, I met Natedogg (my husband). Risks are not comfortable. Outcomes cannot be guaranteed, but risks are worth it. What risk will you take?

BECOMING A PERSON OF ACTION

In our work as educators over almost two decades, we have found some key ways our students work to improve themselves and their lives. It was hard to narrow down, but, on the following page we have shared our top ten list of strategies that have led to our ability to dream big and become people of action. Just like unlocking your potential, we have found when you focus on one of these things at a time, they tend to build on each other and you adopt more of them over time. Remember, when you are on a journey to become the best version of yourself, it starts with taking one step and then another. Results will not be immediate but they will come.

TOP 10 WAYS TO BECOME A PERSON OF ACTION

 Incorporate daily journaling and reflection opportunities. Set aside a consistent time each day to do this.

 "Own your nerd." Be yourself and don't conform to what others want you to be. You are wonderfully made to be yourself.

 Focus on gratitude and joy in all things and circumstances. Commit to daily gratitude practices to keep yourself in the mindset of gratefulness.

 Participate in a Kindness Challenge. Focusing on bringing joy to others through intentional acts of kindness.

 Understand the connection between moving your body, remaining in motion, and the ability to be a person of action mentally.

 Engage in positive visualization. For each task of your day, create a visual picture in your head of things going positively. When you do this, you set yourself on a path to notice the positive blessings you experience throughout your day.

 Establish a healthy routine. What are the activities during the day you want to prioritize? Intentionally schedule them into your daily routine.

 Feed your mind. Consider your food, reading, activities, and social media. How do these experiences help or hinder you?

 Rest, rejuvenation, and the importance of recharging. We can't say enough about getting at least a full eight hours of sleep nightly. Prioritizing down-time and recovering is essential to moving forward and honoring your body.

 Communicate honestly and respectfully. Monitor your impact on others.

FINAL ASSIGNMENT:
WRITE A LETTER TO YOUR FUTURE SELF

This is your time to take all you are learning about yourself and apply it. Write a letter to yourself twenty years in the future. Use the following prompts.

Describe the pieces of yourself you have discovered so far.

Tell your future self what you need to do now to continue to grow.

Explain what it means for you to be true to yourself.

Encourage yourself to embrace the courage you have within you, to continue to work on The Puzzle of You.

....

....

....

....

....

....

....

....

....

....

....

....

....

....

ABOUT THE AUTHORS

Kasia Gutierrez and Christa Pruss are not just educator colleagues; they are also best friends and Confidence Coaches 4 Kids. Together, they have hosted book studies for middle school students, co-taught 6th grade Math and Language Arts, and are aspiring Youtube stars... (in their heads). In addition to supporting kids, they also provide support and resources for teachers, with a focus on Social and Emotional Learning, ensuring ALL students are valued. Kasia is an elementary school principal, leading in her community of Hillsboro Oregon, with her husband Jay and two boys, Jackson and Carter. Christa is a former teacher turned Behavior Specialist, who doesn't just teach, but performs while encouraging her students to "own their nerd." She is also in Hillsboro Oregon with her husband Nate and three kids, Isabelle, Katelyn and Jeffrey.

TO LEARN MORE, VISIT
CONFIDENCECOACHES4KIDS.ORG.